This SpongeBob SquarePants
Annual belongs to:

NICKELODEON™

SPONGEBOB

SQUAREPANTS™

ANNUAL 2010

Contents

EGMONT

We bring stories to life

First published in Great Britain in 2009 by Egmont UK Limited,
239 Kensington High Street, London W8 6SA.

Created For Egmont by Ruby Shoes Ltd
Written by Brenda Apsley   Designed by Graham Wise

© 2009 Viacom International Inc. All Rights Reserved.
Nickelodeon, SpongeBob SquarePants and all related titles, logos and characters
are trademarks of Viacom International Inc. Created by Stephen Hillenburg.

ISBN 978 1 4052 4640 8
1 3 5 7 9 10 8 6 4 2
Printed in Italy

Watch every day on Nickelodeon!
www.nick.co.uk

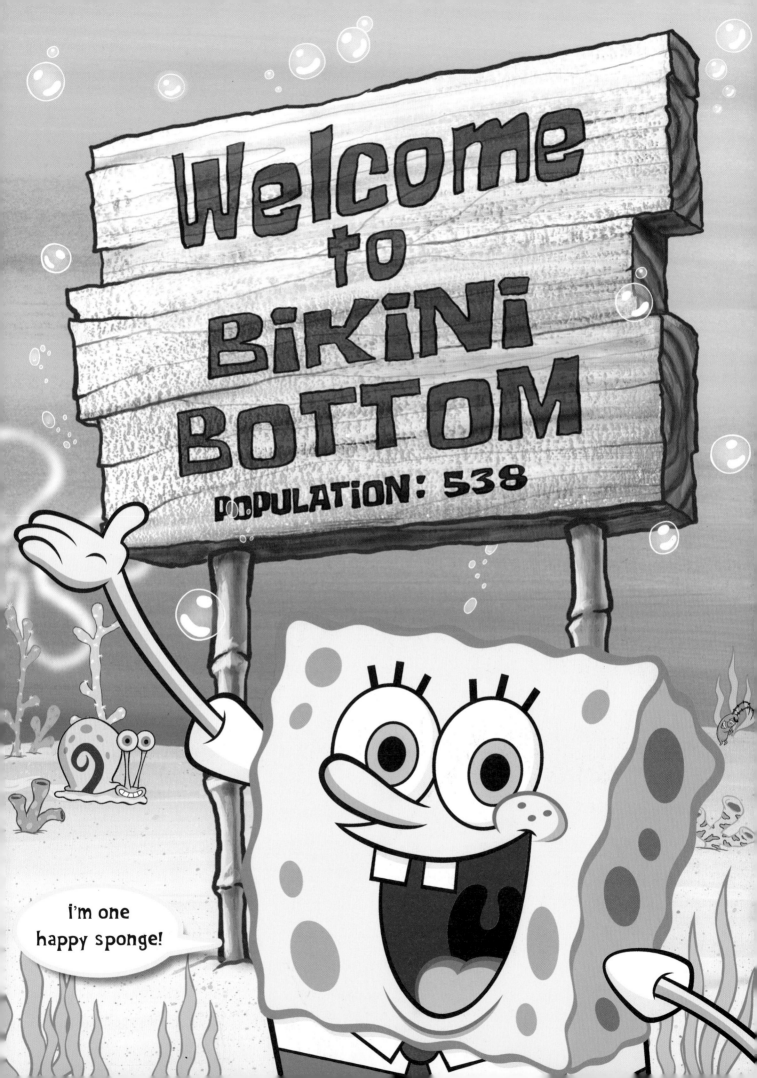

Bikini Bottom

Up Close

Let's take a look around the undersea city ...

124 Conch Street is the two-bedroom pineapple house that yellow sea sponge **SpongeBob SquarePants** calls home. He shares it with his pet snail, **Gary.**

SpongeBob's dream is to pass his boat driving test at Mrs Puff's Boating School, but he has failed it **1,258,056** times. In one desperate try to get his licence, SpongeBob had a walkie-talkie planted in his head so that his friend Patrick could guide him in secret. But he still failed ...

Miaow!

What does SpongeBob lift to keep fit?
Tick ✓ the correct answer.

a

b

c

ANSWER: c, soft toys.

A pink starfish called **Patrick Star** lives under a Rock at 120 Conch Street.

On Best Friends' Day, Patrick gave SpongeBob his most prized possession: an enormous ball of **chewing gum.** Used chewing gum. Complete with mouldy pizza and a smelly sock.

Hey, that's what friends are for!

Go away! I don't like you!

A miserable octopus called **Squidward Tentacles** lives at 122 Conch Street, in Tiki Head House.

Squidward plays (bad) clarinet with the Bikini Bottom Orchestra and is not very friendly ...

Patrick Star
Rock
_124_ Conch Street
Bikini Bottom

Squidward Tentacles
Tiki Head House
_122_ Conch Street
Bikini Bottom

Write house numbers to complete the addresses.

ANSWERS: Patrick lives at 120 and Squidward at 122.

Around Town

The Anchor House is where **Mr Eugene Krabs** lives with his whale-of-a-daughter, **Pearl.** Mr Krabs loves money ... making money, stroking money, stacking money, sorting money, hiding money, saving money, smelling money, counting money. What he doesn't like is spending it!

When SpongeBob gave Mr Krabs a new mattress and got rid of the old one, he fainted, because all his money was hidden in it!

Help Mr Krabs count his money. Write a total in each box.

 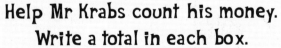 12 $ 10

The Treedome is where karate-kicking, all-action Texan squirrel **Sandy Cheeks** lives.

SpongeBob has a huge crush on Sandy, and he's always trying to impress her. When Sandy helped SpongeBob train for the Mussel Beach body building event, SpongeBob thought all that exercise was too much – so he bought a pair of fake muscle arms to wear.

Yee-haaaa!

True or False?
Tick ✓ or cross ✗ each fact.

ⓐ Sandy is a gerbil.

ⓑ Sandy is from Tahiti.

ⓒ SpongeBob loves Sandy.

ANSWERS: 1. False, she's a squirrel; 2. False, she's from Texas; 3. True, he sure does!

Krusty Krab versus

The **Krusty Krab** is Mr Krabs' lobster pot fast-food joint.

SpongeBob works there as a fry cook, flipping hundreds of the top-secret-recipe Krabby Patties that have made Mr Krabs a very rich crustacean.

SpongeBob loves his job so much that when he was **1 minute** late one morning he moved in to the Krusty Krab so it wouldn't happen again.

It's me pleasure to take yer money!

TODAY'S SPECIALS

A S E
_ _ _ SODAS

Y U K R S T
_ _ _ _ _ _ KELP

H S I F
_ _ _ _ FRIES

Unscramble the white letters to complete the Krusty Krab specials menu.

ANSWERS: the specials are:
SEA SODAS, KRUSTY KELP and FISH FRIES.

Chum Bucket

Sheldon Plankton is the mean, green and microscopic owner of the **Chum Bucket**, the worst eating place in the world. Plankton's only hope of attracting customers is to steal Mr Krabs' Krabby Patty recipe, and this is what he plans to do, aided by his huge family.

Once, Plankton hid out in SpongeBob's head and took control of his **brain.** It took a sponge of unusual sponginess to withstand handing over the secret recipe ...

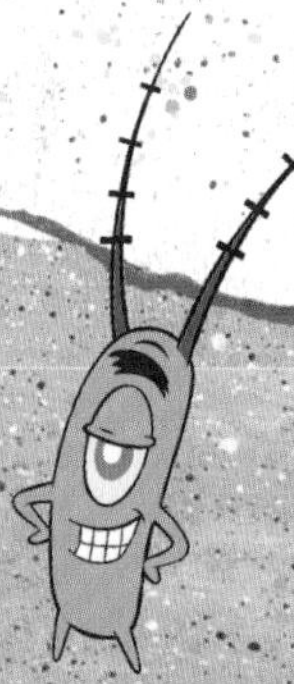

How many of the Plankton clan can you spot in this picture? Write the number.

7

ANSWER: there are 7 of Plankton's relatives.

SpongeBob SquarePants

The Big Race

Panel 1: Just a little further...

Panel 2: Ahh... that's the stretch.

Panel 3: Hey, Squidward!

Yaah!

Panel 4: What are you doing?

I was in a deep stretch, SpongeBob! Don't sneak up on someone in a deep stretch!

Panel 5: I could've pulled something!

Panel 6: And that might have cost me the blue ribbon!

Panel 7: The blue ribbon?

Yes! For tomorrow's Bikini Bottom marathon!

Panel 8: I've been training for months for this run!

Panel 9: If I win, my picture will be in the paper! Everyone will know 'Squidward Tentacles' in Bikini Bottom!

I'll be famous.

Story, art & lettering: Graham Annable. Colour: Wes Dzioba. SpongeBob SquarePants created by Stephen Hillenburg.

That sounds nifty, Squidward. Would you like a Coral Pop?

No!

My body is a finely tuned machine! I can't be just putting junk into it!

The next day.

START

Welcome, folks! We're at the starting line for this year's Bikini Bottom marathon! Let's go meet some of the contestants, shall we? Exciting!

Hello there, sir. How are you feeling about this exciting race today?

Can't talk... conserving all energy.

312

Ha, ha! That's great! Just great! Let's move along here! Amazing!

312

I can't wait to do the real race!

I can't wait to eat a Coral pop!

Hey, SpongeBob! I just saw Squidward's number on the ground!

Really?

Gosh, you're right, Patrick!

We've got to get this to him so he's ready for the real race!

When are we gonna have our Coral pops?

There's the finish line!

Just got to push it a little further, then--

Hey Squidward! Look what I have!

Yaaa!

We found your number on the--

GIVE ME THAT!

GIVE IT!

HA!

Hey, look!

SpongeBob won the warm-up race!

Amazing finish!

Later...

Hey, Squidward! You want a Coral pop?

I didn't know I got a lifetime supply for winning!

Gaaah.

End.

Spot the Difference

SpongeBob just loves his job at the Krusty Krab – even the cleaning up!
These pictures look the same, but **10** things are different in picture **2**. Can you spot them all?

Whoa!

Tra-la-lah!

Puzzled with Patrick

Patrick loves puzzle stuff, but he's not much good at puzzle stuff, so can you help?

Prize Photo

This photo won First Prize at the Bikini Bottom Camera Club Show.
Can you guess the title?

Patrick (hey, that's me!)
As Seen from Pluto.

Spelling Bee

Which word is always spelt wrongly?

is it
r-o-n-g-l-y?

How Long ...

is a piece of string?

Errrr?

You got him, Sponge-Bob!

Just one more step!

Oof!

What is that?

I don't know, Patrick.

An old case?

With horns!

Maybe it's an ancient horned pirate suitcase!

Full of horned pirate booty!

Hey, can pirate booty be haunted, Sponge-Bob?

M-maybe... if it's old enough.

Story: Graham Annable. Colour: Wes Dzioba. SpongeBob SquarePants created by Stephen Hillenburg.

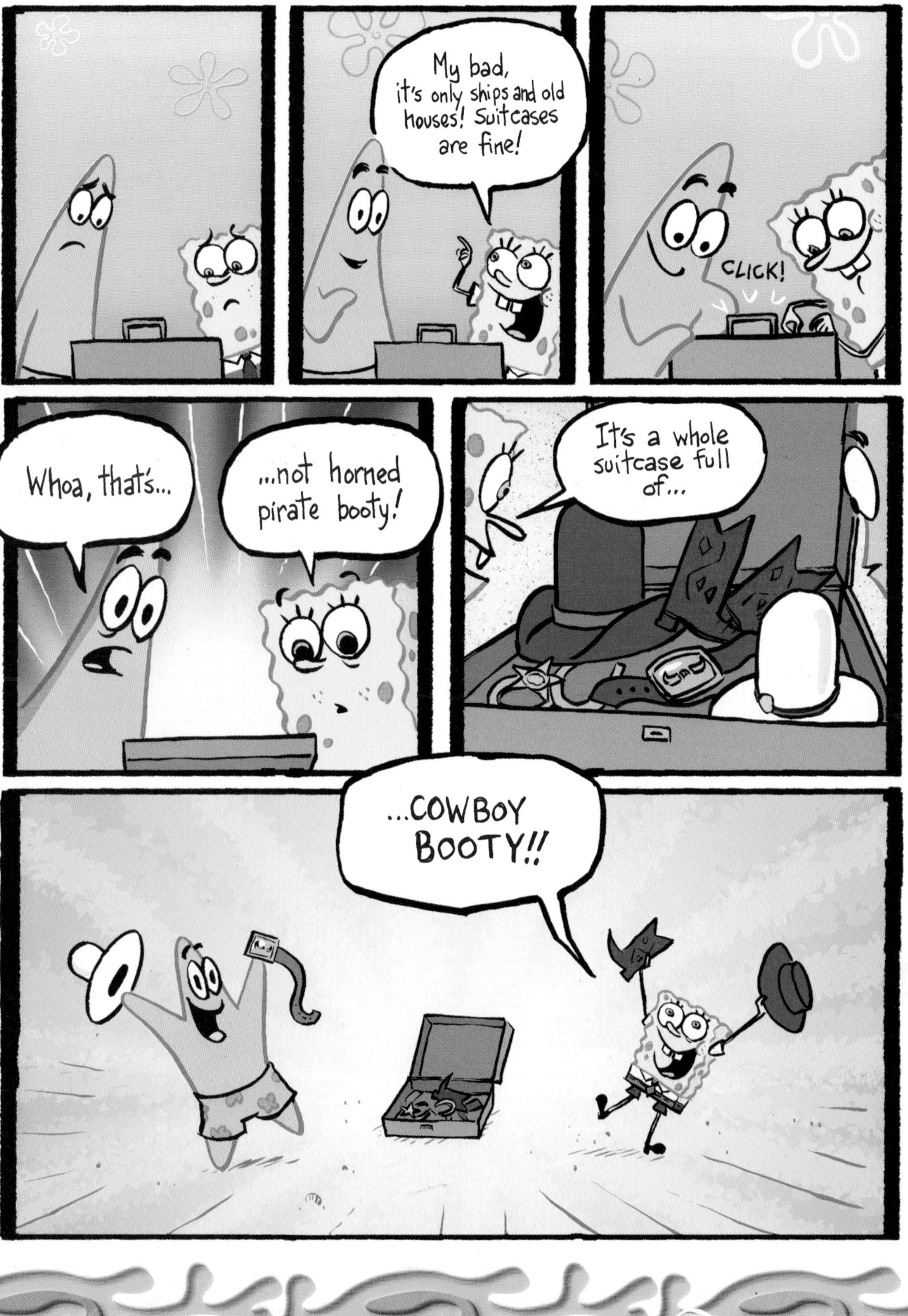
My bad, it's only ships and old houses! Suitcases are fine!
CLICK!
Whoa, that's...
...not horned pirate booty!
It's a whole suitcase full of...
...COWBOY BOOTY!!

SpongeBob SnailPark

Story: David Lewman. Pencils: Gregg Schigiel. Inks: Jeff Albrecht. Colour: SnoCone Studios. Lettering: Comicraft. SpongeBob SquarePants created by Stephen Hillenburg.

GARY, DON'T STEAL THEIR TOYS!

GARY, DON'T FORCE THEM TO PERFORM IN A SNAIL CIRCUS!

I THOUGHT YOU WANTED TO BE WITH OTHER--

SNAP!

MEAN SNAILS ARE NOT WELCOME HERE!

BUT GARY ISN'T MEAN... USUALLY.

JUST TAKE YOUR BULLY AND GO, BAD OWNER!

SNAIL BOARD

WAIT! THAT'S NOT WHAT YOU WANTED...

NOW THIS IS THE RIGHT PARK FOR GARY! YEAH! CARVE IT UP!

MEOW!

THE END.

SPONGEBOB SQUAREPANTS™

SpongeBob E.V.I.L. Pants

THAT'S RIGHT, PATRICK! I, SPONGEBOB SQUAREPANTS, HAVE DECIDED TO JOIN THE FORCES OF *E.V.I.L.*!

GASP!

YOU MEAN...?

YES, EVERY VILLAIN *IS* IN *E.V.I.L.*, THE GANG OF SUPER BAD GUYS!

OH, SPONGEBOB! WHY? WHY?!

DON'T WORRY, PATRICK. I'M NOT *REALLY* TURNING EVIL. I'M JUST GOING UNDERCOVER!

Story: David Lewman. Pencils: Gregg Schigiel. Inks: Jeff Albrecht. Colour: Wes Dzioba. Lettering: Comicraft. SpongeBob SquarePants created by Stephen Hillenburg.

BUT WHY ARE YOU DRESSED LIKE SUCH A WEIRDO?

TO JOIN *E.V.I.L.*, YOU HAVE TO BE A SUPERVILLAIN.

AND SO I AM... *THE LITTLE LITTERER!*

SEE? *E.V.I.L.'S* HOLDING TRYOUTS TODAY.

CAN I COME, TOO?

BE E.V.I.L.

OH, NO, MY GENTLE FRIEND. IT'S FAR TOO DANGEROUS.

GOOD.

THESE APPLICANTS HAD BETTER BE GOOD--I MEAN *EVIL.*

WE GOTTA GET MORE VILLAINS TO PULL OFF THE BIG HEIST!

C'MON, WE'VE ONLY RENTED THE GYM UNTIL NOON. *ENTER!*

DIRTY BUBBLE

MAN RAY

JUMBO SHRIMP

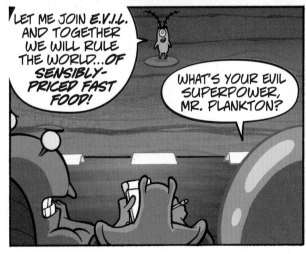

LET ME JOIN *E.V.I.L.* AND TOGETHER WE WILL RULE THE WORLD...OF SENSIBLY-PRICED FAST FOOD!

WHAT'S YOUR EVIL SUPERPOWER, MR. PLANKTON?

MY EVIL LAUGH! *BWHA-HA-HA-HA!*

WE WANT TO BE TAKEN SERIOUSLY. REJECTED!

PLEASE ACCEPT THIS EVIL BACKSCRATCHER AS A CONSOLATION PRIZE.

40

FINALLY...

UM, EXCUSE ME, IS THIS WHERE THE *E.V.I.L.* TRYOUTS ARE?

YES, YOU DOLT!

HURRY! IT'S ALMOST NOON, AND WE HAVE A LOT OF VILLAINS TO SEE!

ACTUALLY, I'M THE LAST ONE. THE OTHERS ALL PUSHED IN FRONT OF ME.

FINE.

JUST SHOW US WHAT YOU GOT.

OKAY, JUST A SECOND. GOTTA GET IN CHARACTER...

...

BEHOLD! TIS I, THE LITTLE LITTERER!

AND WHAT IS YOUR SUPERPOWER, MR. LITTERER?

JUST WATCH!

WHEN MY HELPLESS VICTIMS LEAST EXPECT IT, I...

...LITTER!

HA! HA! HA! HA! HA!

THAT'S IT? LITTERING?

CONSIDER YOURSELF REJECTED!

PLEASE ACCEPT THIS PIECE OF LITTER AS A CONSOLATION PRIZE.

BUT... BUT I REALLY WANTED TO JOIN...

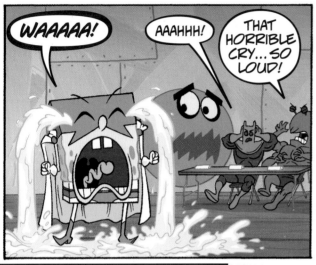

WAAAAA!

AAAHHH!

THAT HORRIBLE CRY... SO LOUD!

OKAY, KID, YOU'RE IN!

ALL THESE TEARS! I'M GETTING CLEAN!

NOW *THIS* IS A SUPERPOWER WE CAN USE!

I AM?

SOON, AT E.V.I.L. HEADQUARTERS...

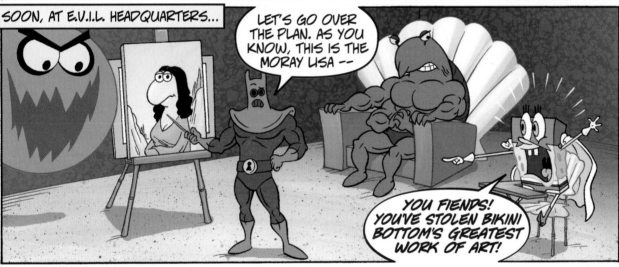

LET'S GO OVER THE PLAN. AS YOU KNOW, THIS IS THE MORAY LISA --

YOU FIENDS! YOU'VE STOLEN BIKINI BOTTOM'S GREATEST WORK OF ART!

THIS IS A DRAWING! WE HAVEN'T STOLEN THE *REAL* ONE YET!

OH. RIGHT. PLEASE CONTINUE.

INSIDE THE MUSEUM, DIRTY BUBBLE WILL USE HIS AWESOME POWERS TO HOLD THE GUARD. I'LL ZAP THE LOCK WITH MY AWESOME EVIL RAY. AND JUMBO SHRIMP WILL CARRY THE PAINTING WITH HIS AWESOME STRENGTH.

AWESOME!

WHAT'LL I DO?

WELL, BIG CRYBABY...

THAT'S LITTLE LITTERER.

...YOU'LL CRY TO DISTRACT THE MUSEUM'S VISITORS.

Happy, happy Happy

Jellyfishing. Bubble blowing. Riding on fishing hooks. SpongeBob and Patrick can always find reasons to be happy.

"To be happy as a clam," says SpongeBob, "you just have to ..."

Think happy!

~~Hippy!~~ ~~Hoppy!~~ **Happy!**

How many times is the word **HAPPY** spelled out in the bubbles?

Draw a line through each one, then count them and write the number.

12

H	A	P	P	Y	H	J	L
A	X	U	O	H	A	M	K
P	E	T	H	A	P	P	Y
P	V	H	A	P	P	Y	H
Y	H	A	P	P	Y	G	A
H	A	P	P	Y	B	O	P
C	W	P	Y	R	F	Q	P
A	S	Y	H	A	P	P	Y

ANSWER: the word 'HAPPY' appears 12 times.

46

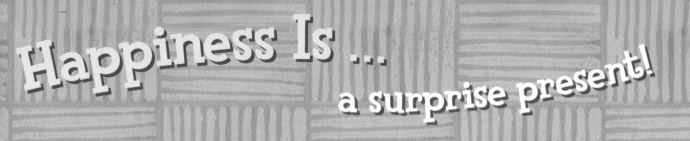

Happiness Is ...
a surprise present!

What do you give the sponge who has everything? **You decide!** Draw and colour in a surprise gift to make SpongeBob happy, and write your name on the gift tag.

To SpongeBob From

Sock Troubles

Story, art & lettering: Graham Annable. Colour: Wes Dzioba. SpongeBob SquarePants created by Stephen Hillenburg.

SPONGEY Secrets

Here are some of SpongeBob's most **TOP-SECRET** secrets. But a word is missing from each one.

Choose the correct word from the opposite page to complete each secret, and write the number in each porthole.

a To earn some extra cash, SpongeBob sold ...

door to door.

b SpongeBob likes to put ...

on both sides of his toast.

c At the zoo, SpongeBob made an oyster cry when he tossed a ...

Pear

at it.

OYSTER STADIUM

BIKINI BOTTOM ZOO

1 jellyfish jelly

2 chocolate bars

3 squirrels

4 Ol' Buzzy

5 Gary

6 peanut

7 pickle

SpongeBob called his favourite jellyfish ...

SpongeBob went on strike when a customer said there was no ...

on his Krabby Patty.

SpongeBob became a comedy star when he told jokes about ...

SpongeBob was taught to tie his shoelaces by...

Patrick's Sleepover

Story: David Lewman. Pencils: Gregg Schigiel. Inks: Jeff Albrecht. Colour: SnoCone Studios. Letters: ComicraFt. SpongeBob SquarePants created by Stephen Hillenburg.

HOW COME YOU GET THREE MATTRESSES, AND I HAVE TO SLEEP ON THE FLOOR?

YOU'RE RIGHT!

AS THE GUEST, YOU SHOULD GET THE BED.

COMFY NOW?

NOPE.

NOW?

NOPE.

NOW?

NOPE.

I DON'T GET IT.

WE STARFISH ARE EXCELLENT SLEEPERS. I'VE PERSONALLY WON MANY PROFESSIONAL COMPETITIONS.

I'VE GOT IT!

SLEEP WELL, MY FRIEND!

ZZZZZ...

THE END

Put on your superhero cape and help find the hiding places of *8* of the Plankton clan. You might need this, too!

You found all *8?* Then here's your SpongeBob superhero badge. Colour it in – and wear with pride!

Full Moon FEVER

Story & pencils: Gregg Schigiel. Inks: Jeff Albrecht. Colours: Comicraft. Lettering: Wes Dzioba. SpongeBob SquarePants created by Stephen Hillenburg.

OH, NO! MR. KRABS, COME QUICK!

SHIVER ME TIMBERS! ME KITCHEN LOOKS LIKE A SHIPWRECK!

SOMEONE MUST HAVE BROKEN IN LAST NIGHT AND MADE A MESS OF EVERYTHING!

≡YAWN≡ WHAT HAPPENED HERE?

YER LATE! THAT'S WHAT HAPPENED HERE.

LOOK, THERE'S HALF-EATEN, UNCOOKED KRABBY PATTIES EVERYWHERE!

WHY WOULD ANYBODY--

BURP!

YUCK! WHAT'S THAT TASTE IN MY MOUTH?

IT TASTES LIKE...

OH, NO.

WHAT D'YEH FIGURE SQUIDWARD IS UP TO?

GARY SAYS HE GOT A NEW PET DOGFISH.

MAYBE HE FORGOT TO FEED IT?

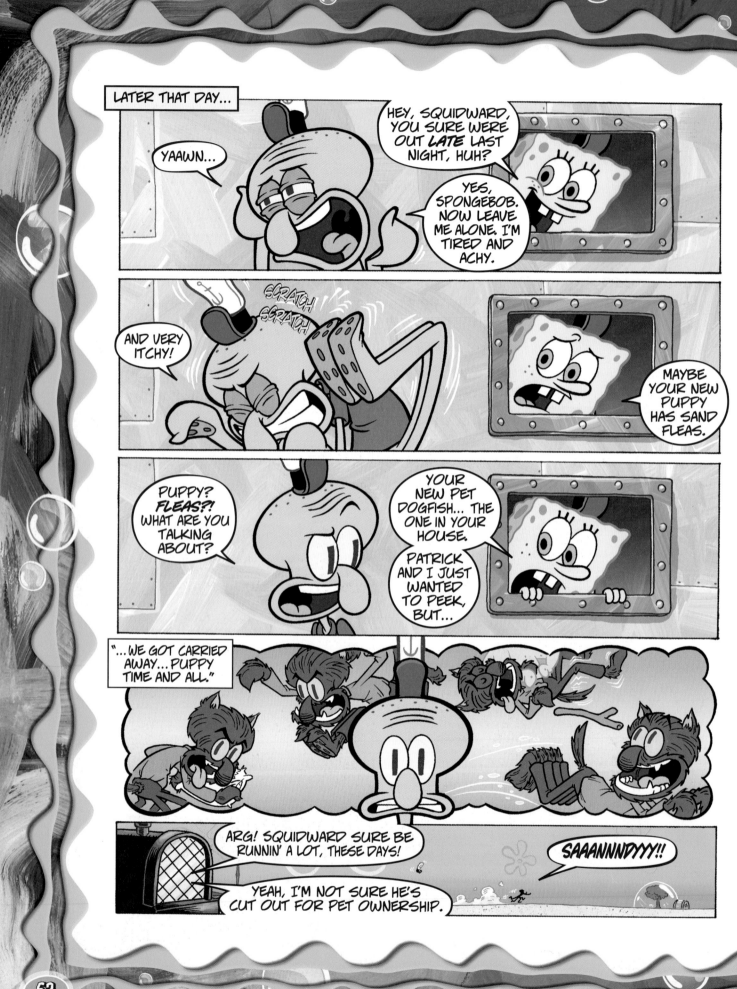

YOU'VE **GOT** TO HELP ME! I WAS BITTEN BY A HOWLER, AND NOW EVERY NIGHT I TURN **INTO** ONE!

EVEN **WORSE**, I'M EATING RAW KRABBY PATTIES AND GETTING BELLY RUBS FROM PATRICK AND FETCHING STICKS FOR SPONGEBOB AND--

HOLD YER SEAHORSES, SQUIDWARD!

SOUNDS T'ME LIKE YA GOT A CASE OF **FULL MOON FEVER**, AND Y'ALL'S GOT IT BAD.

GOOD THING I KNOW THE FIX. JUST WAIT AT HOME AND I'LL BE BY...

"...LATER."

DING DONG

OH, WHERE'S SANDY WITH THAT CURE!?

SANDY, YOU'RE HERE! THANK GOODNESS!

YEP, AND I BRUNG A CURE FER YER HOWLER PROBLEM!

BAKED BEANS?!?

SURE! EVERYBODY KNOWS THE CURE FER THE HOWLERISM IS SIXTEEN BOWLS OF BAKED BEANS!

AND IT'S JUST A FEW HOURS TILL MOONLIGHT, SO YA BEST GET A MOVE ON!

≥GAG≤

THE END

Food Fight

Story & art: Graham Annable. Colour: Wes Dzioba. SpongeBob SquarePants created by Stephen Hillenburg.

SpongeBob SquarePants

Permanent Bubbles

PUFF...
PUFFFF...
P-P-PUFF!

I DID IT!

PATRICK, QUICK! I FINALLY BLEW A BUBBLE OF KING NEPTUNE RIDING HIS--

POP!

HI, SPONGEBOB! WHAT DID YOU WANT TO SHOW ME?

OH, NOTHING...

I LOVE BLOWING BUBBLES. BUT THEY POP BEFORE I CAN SHOW THEM TO ANYONE.

MAYBE I CAN INVENT SOMETHIN' TO HELP...

JUST SPRAY YER BUBBLES WITH THIS, AND THEY'LL NEVER POP.

WOW! THANKS, SANDY!

SPONGEBOB!!!

END

Story: David Lewman. Pencils: Gregg Schigiel. Inks: Jeff Albrecht. Colour: Wes Dzioba. Lettering: ComicraFt. SpongeBob SquarePants created by Stephen Hillenburg.

Byeee!

Crack SpongeBob's coded message by writing the letter for each symbol.

A B C D E F G H I J K L M N

O P Q R S T U V W X Y Z

L i F e

I s   s w e l l !